What's In It For Me?
1 ~ *Answering That Question* ~ 1

by
David K. Ewen, M.Ed.

What's In It For Me?
Answering That Question
By
David K. Ewen, M.Ed.

ISBN-13: 978-1493640737

ISBN-10: 1493640739

Copyright © 2013, Ewen Prime Company

ALL RIGHTS RESERVED. This book contains material protected under International and Federal Copyright Laws and Treaties. Any unauthorized reprint or use of this material is prohibited. No part of this book may be reproduced or transmitted in any form or by any means, electronic or mechanical, including photocopying, recording, or by any information storage and retrieval system without express written permission from Ewen Prime Company, Inc.

What's In It For Me?
~ *Answering That Question* ~

by
David K. Ewen, M.Ed.

Dedication

This book is dedicated to all of my students over the years who eventually became published, recorded, or broadcasted and were able to present themselves successfully in front of the media and in turn made their content successfully marketed. Those are the students who took advantage of the marketing model presented in my lectures resulting in their success. My goal has always been to see my student's success. For that I am grateful.

What's In It For Me?
3 ~ *Answering That Question* ~ 3

by
David K. Ewen, M.Ed.

Appreciation

Since 2004, I have lectured in the seven states of New York and New England on marketing content that is published, recorded, and broadcasted. On many school, college, and university campuses, my beautiful wife Maria has accompanied me for support and companionship. Over those many years and many more to come, Maria has seen me lecture on the specific marketing topics discussed in this book. She has witnessed the final discovery, development, and final production of the copyrighted marketing model

   WIIFM=(It/This) will (Make/Give) you _X_. (Copyright © 2006, Ewen Prime Co.)

Maria knows very well what it means and how to use it. She was there when it was developed. Maria has served as my first audience to test if this model makes sense. Once a lecture approach did make sense, she knew it could be explained and then practiced in the workplace and general market. My wife, Maria has seen it all.

The marketing model presented in this book was developed with Maria alongside. I appreciate the fact that I wasn't alone and she was the one who witnessed the development of something so very important that crosses so many genre of industry. I focus my use on the model for content delivery in publishing, recording, and broadcasting.

So to my beautiful wife Maria, I say thank you for being part of business as it is so very important not to be alone when something new is born. This little baby is ours and not mine alone. *"Honey, I love you."*

What's In It For Me?
4 ~ *Answering That Question* ~ 4

by
David K. Ewen, M.Ed.

About The Author

Professor David K. Ewen, M.Ed. is an author, speaker, writer, consultant, and adjunct lecturer on new digital media technologies in publishing, film, radio, television, webcasting, business, economics, marketing, and publicity. A portfolio of written and published that demonstrates experience can be found at **www.ForestAcademy.org** David has also worked in broadcasting since 1994 beginning in radio at WORC 1310 AM and WGFP 940 AM. He has filmed and produced several shows for community public access television. David's talents are both technical and creative. Since 2004, David has been lecturing on the topics of new digital multimedia technologies in the seven states of New York and New England. David researches, develops, writes, and publishes his lectures.

What's In It For Me?
5 ~ *Answering That Question* ~ 5

by
David K. Ewen, M.Ed.

Introduction

The marketing model presented here is one third of the total marketing package. When I lecture on college campuses on the topic of marketing I first talk about the difference between marketing and publicity. Some businesses make the mistake of using those words and functionality interchangeable. Marketing and publicity are two very different entities. Marketing is what you say when selling. It is content that is used for selling. Publicity is the delivery of that marketing content. For example marketing is an ad that goes in a newspaper. The newspaper delivery is the publicity. My discussion of marketing will not be a discussion of broadcasting or social media or commercials.

Putting our focus on marketing and not publicity, let me announce what is in this book. A marketing model that I copyrighted several years ago has three elements to it. I will be talking about one of them in this book as it is the most challenging. What is being discussed here was copyrighted in 2006. The combination of all three was copyrighted in 2012.

I chose to write this book to put more focus and attention of the most challenging element of the three part marketing model. It can serve standalone from the other two elements. It is also the most important as it serves as a communication and way of thinking with your client or customer.

What's In It For Me?
6 ~ *Answering That Question* ~ 6

by
David K. Ewen, M.Ed.

Introduction continued ...

What is described here is easy to explain, but hard to do. Why? Because our brains aren't wired to think this way. Our natural subconscious thinking steers us away from effective marketing. Most businesses know that. I've developed a tool to act as a set of train tracks to go along so that you can be more effective in your marketing efforts.

Once you understand what this book explains, it will take practice. The book is short, but the practice is long. Don't take the basic understanding for granted. The practice you do will pay off. Failing to practice is lazy. Laziness is part of that subconscious thinking that directs us toward th path of least resistance. You need to force yourself through that resistance to be accustomed to effective marketing. Effective marketing requires doing something that isn't natural to you because it requires anticipating another person's interests, desires, satisfaction rather than your own.

so again, it's a short book, but the practice is long.

What's In It For Me?
7 ~ *Answering That Question* ~ 7

by
David K. Ewen, M.Ed.

History

There are fancy workshop seminars held in big hotel conference centers costing thousands of dollars and lasting for several days to teach people how to explain to a client or customer the value of their product or service. As a media specialist since 1994, I have had many sleepless nights trying to figure out how to accomplish the same goal, but without the cost. It took about fifteen years to figure it out and another five to prove that what I figured out works. I've boiled it down to one sentence. It's easy to explain, but hard to do because it differs from our natural way of thinking. Rather than go to the week long expensive seminar, take this book and do as instructed. Maintain the practice and you'll be successful.

What's In It For Me?
8 ~ *Answering That Question* ~ 8

by
David K. Ewen, M.Ed.

Yourself

Think of yourself as a consumer. If you were in a crowded room and everyone was asked the question where they go food shopping, you'll discover that people tend to favor different stores for different reasons. We all need to eat, however there are choices that provide the same basic food. What store do you shop for food? Think of the reason. Would it be the same reason for anyone, or would someone else pick another store for a reason that is perceived to be more important. Perhaps it is for the same reason, however the selection of choice is different. For example, suppose you go to one store because it is near to you. Another person may go to another store for the same reason, however the other store is near him or her.

Now think of your product or service. You aren't the only one with that product or service. Your clients or customers make a choice just like you make a choice of where to shop for food. What is it you can say about your product or service that give interest to your client or customer. What about your competitors? What will they say? What will put you on top? That's what this book is about. Putting you on top.

What's In It For Me?
9 ~ *Answering That Question* ~ 9

by
David K. Ewen, M.Ed.

Marketing Element Model

This is the marketing element model that will be discussed in this book. It may not make sense now, but it will become clear as we go over each of the circled items.

After this model has been clearly identified, it will then be time to practice.

I show the model up front, so was we build the concept of what it means and how to use it, you'll have a picture in mind.

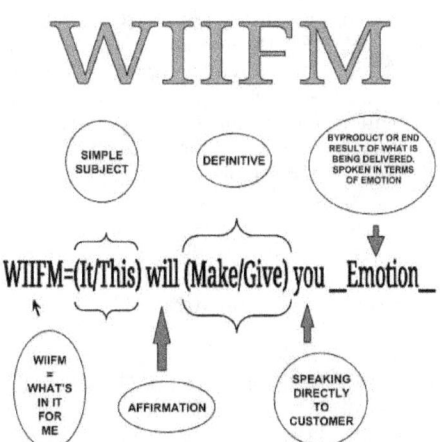

What's In It For Me?
10 ~ *Answering That Question* ~ 10

by
David K. Ewen, M.Ed.

Premise

When people are given a choice to select from, the natural response is to ask, "What's in it for me". We abbreviate this standard client/customer question by calling it WIIFM (What's In It For Me?). In one form or another, that is what your client or customer is asking. Dig deeper, and you will find that in most cases, a lower price is not what they are looking for. A reason may be convenience or comfort that will override a lower price value. That being said, the value a client or customer perceives is given a value. If the value equates to or is larger than the price, then satisfaction will be met.

So the question to you is, how do you explain value to the client or customer? There are five points to the effective answer the the customer's question "What's In It For Me" (WIIFM). Below is a summary, but in the following pages, we will go over some more detail.

- **BREVITY**: Speak with brevity and to the point
- **AFFIRMATION**: Affirmation with confidence and not hesitancy
- **DEFINITIVE**: Definitive action verb demonstrating anticipated results
- **CUSTOMER**: Speak directly to the customer instead of a general audience
- **HEART**: Talking to the customer's heart to evoke emotion. Not their head

What's In It For Me?
11 ~ *Answering That Question* ~ 11

by
David K. Ewen, M.Ed.

Brevity

The answer to WIIFM (What's In It For Me?) needs to be brief. People remember less than half of what you tell them. Keeping it short increases the probability, that not only are you heard, but you are listened to. Being heard is the recognition of noise. Listening involves the paying attention. If you are brief and to the point, your client or customer will more likely remember what you are telling him or her.

Imagine a one hour classroom lecture. What would happen if you didn't take notes? How much will you remember? When you speak to your customer, they usually aren't taking notes. Being direct, simple, and to the point in one sentence with the right element will get your point across.

Remember. Get to the point. Be aware people forget most of what you tell them. They won't be able to recite it. That being said, make your words count. It's not how much you say, but what you say. People with few words can make a huge impact.

The good thing, is this book provides you the tool to ensure you are brief. However, it must be practiced.

What's In It For Me?
12 ~ *Answering That Question* ~ 12

by
David K. Ewen, M.Ed.

Affirmation

The answer to WIIFM (What's In It For Me) must evoke a confident affirmation. A customer can recognize if there is a loss in confidence if you mistakenly talk about your product or service in terms of "perhaps", "potential", "Should", "might", "Could", "Maybe",   These words are used subconsciously and therefore accidently.   Those types of words will immediately lose the trust of a customer.   If you don't have true trust in yourself, then what comes out of your mouth will show it.

There is one word to use. It is the word "Will". Imagine the language that talks about what your product or service will do rather than should, or could do.   Using the word "will" is confident and non arguable. The other words like "perhaps", "potential", "Should", "might", "Could", "Maybe" results in questions. You don't want those questions to come up. You don't want your product or service to be questionable. Eliminate that by using the word "will". Make the statement and affirmation that your product or service will have a result.   There will be no wondering of what your product or service potential value is.

What's In It For Me?
13   ~ *Answering That Question* ~   13

by
David K. Ewen, M.Ed.

What's In It For Me?
14 ~ *Answering That Question* ~ 14

by
David K. Ewen, M.Ed.

Definative

The answer to WIIFM (What's In It For Me) must have a verb that shows an action evoking confidence rather than a potential. The affirmation "will" is a given. Move forward with the verb and the only two choices toward the positive is "**Make**" or "**Give**". The idea is that your product or service will make something happen or it will give something to happen.

The adverbs "potentially", "possibly" in front of "Make" or "Give" will diffuse the impact you need to have. Once again, a lack of confidence will subconsciously put the words similar to "potentially" and "possibly" out of your mouth. You may not notice it, but your customer or client will. After that, he or she will not have a reason to pay attention any further.

The definitive words help you get to the point. It helps to satisfy the need for brevity. It's a very simple verb to use.

What's In It For Me?
~ *Answering That Question* ~

by
David K. Ewen, M.Ed.

Affirmation & Definative

So let's combine the affirmation previously discussed with the required definitive. The affirmation is the word "Will" that will precede the choice of one of two definitive words "Make" or 'Give". Let's see what it looks like when we combine an affirmation with a definitive when talking about your product or service.

- Will make
- Will give

So your product or service "will make" or "will give". Let's refer to your product or service with either "It" or "This" to help be brief, to the point, and put more focus on the affirmation and definitive.

- It will make
- This will make
- It will give
- This will give

Don't add any other word before the word "will". At this point we are building a sentence that uses a simple subject like "It" or "This" to be brief, to the point, simple, and easy to remember.

What's In It For Me?
16 ~ *Answering That Question* ~ 16

by
David K. Ewen, M.Ed.

Customer

When people are making an effort to relate to their customer and don't have confidence, they'll make the subconscious mistake of relating their product or service to themselves rather than the customer. It is accidental and unnoticed by everyone except most importantly, the customer. This is when the product or service is spoken in terms of what is does for yourself instead of what it does for the customer. It may sound good with the thinking that you believe in the product. It turns out customers really don't care about what the product or service does for you. Remember, they are asking the question (WIIFM) "What's In It For Me?". The moment you don't answer WIIFM is the moment the customer hears, but does not listen. They hear your voice, but putting no true important attention to listen to what you are saying.

To help you put focus on the customer, use the word "You" to have you speak to the customer's needs, satisfaction, and desires. This way, you are really answering "What's In It For Me?". The key word is "Me". That being said, you must use the word "You" in your answer. Never talk about your product or service in terms of yourself. Always put the attention to your client or customer.

What's In It For Me?
~ Answering That Question ~

by
David K. Ewen, M.Ed.

Affirmation & Definitive & Customer

We previously talked about the affirmation and definitive and how they work together. Now let's see what it looks like when we put the focus on the customer. As we did before, we will use the simple subject of "It" or "This" for brevity, simplicity, and keeping to the point.

- It will make you (_blank_)
- This will make you (_blank_)
- It will give you (_blank_)
- This will give you (_blank_)

The only thing remaining is filling in the **blank**. But before we do, take a closer look. It would seem that the blank could be satisfied with one word. By just using a simple subject, affirmation, definitive, and focusing on the customer, we have a sentence that is direct, to the point, assured, positive, and directly answers the question "What's In It For Me?" (WIIFM)

What's In It For Me?
18 ~ *Answering That Question* ~ 18

by
David K. Ewen, M.Ed.

Heart

We have discussed talking directly to your customer, but haven't really talked about in what way. There are two ways. You can talk to someone's head or to their heart. Speaking to the heart is in reference to an emotion.

An example of talking to the "Head" about something is when you say that something is good or nice. An example of talking to someone's "Heart" to evoke emotion is when you say something that will give an emotional effect. For example to indicate something "will make you smile" or "give you nightmares". People tend to remember more of what makes them smile or gives them nightmares instead of being told that something is nice. This is the difference between talking to the head versus talking to the heart.

We previously discussed earlier the importance of an affirmation and definitive and speaking directly to the customer. This combination forces us to speak to the heart and use emotion as a resulting effect. Let's look at our affirmation, definitive, using a simple subject and speaking directly to the customer again.

- It will make you (_blank_)
- This will make you (_blank_)
- It will give you (_blank_)
- This will give you (_blank_)

Now, put an emotion in the place of that blank. Try using one word. You can use up to three, but you would be red-lining it. It is best to use one.

What's In It For Me?
19   ~ *Answering That Question* ~   19

by
David K. Ewen, M.Ed.

What's In It For Me?
20 ~ *Answering That Question* ~ 20

by
David K. Ewen, M.Ed.

Examples

Let's say you are promoting a scary book or movie

- It will make you scream
- This will make you poop your pants
- It will give you chills
- This will give you nightmares

Suppose you were talking about a new ice cream product for the summer.

- It will make you relaxed
- This will make you drool
- It will give you satisfaction
- This will give you excitement

In this example, you wouldn't want to use the word "Cooler" as it is not the best example of evoking and emotion. Although the word "Cooler" in hot weather talks to escaping the heat. Don't let that word "escape" be use either. The word after "you" must be an emotion. So in our example, if we were to think about "cooler" or "escape", what emotion comes out of that? You may consider, depending on the context, words like refuge, safety, protection, relaxation, comfortable. Think about it. Isn't it better to say, "It will make you comfortable" instead of "It will make you cooler"? Think about how the word comfortable is the end product of being cooler. That's what you have to think of. Think of the byproduct and what that emotion might be. That is what people will remember.

What's In It For Me?
~ *Answering That Question* ~

by
David K. Ewen, M.Ed.

Definition

Let's put some formal definition to our answer to the client or customer's question WIIFM, "What's In It For Me?"

WIIFM = (It/This) will (Make/Give) you __(emotion)_

WIIFM represents *"What's In It For Me"*

- Select one of the words "It" or "This" from (It/This) to satisfy the simple subject.

- The word "will" is an affirmation. Do not add a word in between the simple subject and the affirmation.

- Select one of the words "Make" or "Give" from (Make/Give) to satisfy the definitive.

- The last word or two represents the emotion that satisfies the end result of what you give to the customer. The emotion speaks to the customer's heart - not their head. I'll explain more later.

What's In It For Me?
22 ~ *Answering That Question* ~ 22

by
David K. Ewen, M.Ed.

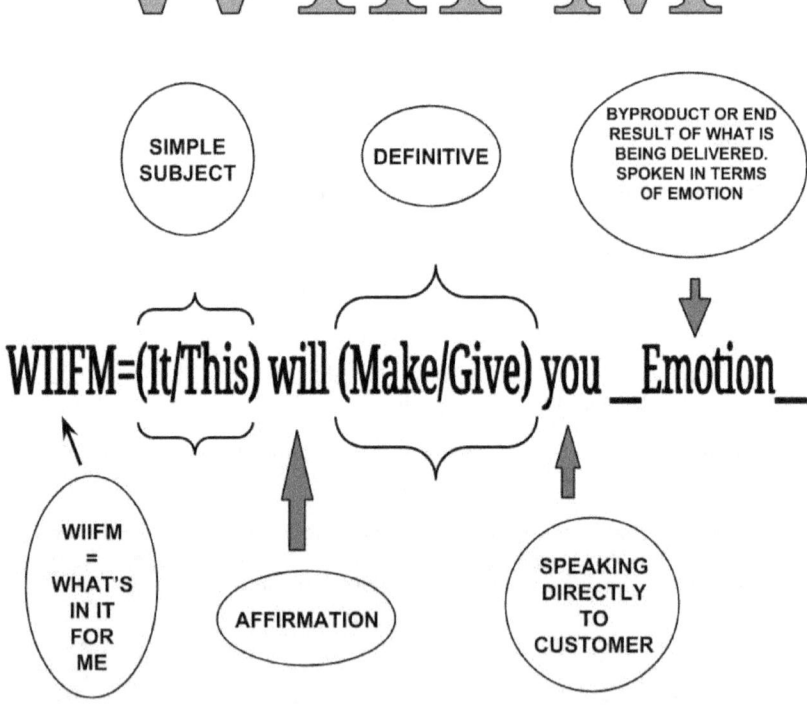

What's In It For Me?
~ *Answering That Question* ~

by
David K. Ewen, M.Ed.

More Examples

Now that we have a model definition, let's do some more practice. Our definition is:

WIIFM = (It/This) will (Make/Give) you __*Emotion*__.   Using this definition, we can answer WIIFM, "What's In It For Me?" in four ways:

- It will make you _*Emotion*_
- This will give you _*Emotion*_
- It will give you _*Emotion*_
- This will make you _*Emotion*_

How about some of these examples:

Example 1
- It will make you patient.
- This will give you patience.
- It will give you appreciation.
- This will make you appreciate.

Example 2
- It will make you relax.
- This will give you relaxation.
- It will give you peace.
- This will make you peaceful.

What's In It For Me?
24 ~ *Answering That Question* ~ 24

by
David K. Ewen, M.Ed.

More on Emotion

In our example below "X" is an emotion, preferably presented as one word.

- It will make you _X_
- This will give you _X_
- It will give you _X_
- This will make you _X_

The emotion **X** is a resulting feeling based on the byproduct or end result of the delivery of your product or service. Is it comfort? Is it a smile? Could it be convenience? Might it be relief? Or perhaps satisfaction. What about revelation? How about some of these other emotions: surprise, wonder, happiness, amusement, courage, pity, pride, closeness, patience, relaxation, envy, fear, respect, appreciation, love, hope, confusion, joy, disgust, trust, shame.

When you are trying to figure out what goes in _X_, keep brief. Instead of saying "It will make you a little sad", try removing the words "a little" and be more direct by saying "It will make you sad".

Here's another example. Instead of saying, "This will make you trust sometimes", try removing the word "sometimes". Either the trust is there or it isn't. Be more direct by saying "This will make you trust".

Whenever possible put more effort on using a single word for the emotional end result of the product or service your are delivering.

What's In It For Me?
25 ~ *Answering That Question* ~ 25

by
David K. Ewen, M.Ed.

Features & Benefits

Let's talk about how discussion features and benefits play a role in our discussion of WIIFM

WIIFM = (It/This) will (Make/Give) you **_Emotion_**.   Using this definition, we can answer WIIFM, "***What's In It For Me?***" in four ways:

- It will make you _Emotion_
- This will give you _Emotion_
- It will give you _Emotion_
- This will make you _Emotion_

A good marketing rule of thumb is to remember the rule "Features Tell & Benefits Sell". For example the feature of a chair is the cushion and the benefit is comfort.   Notice that the benefit is an emotion. In another example the feature of a large car is it's size and the benefit is the relaxation during a long ride. Notice the benefit in the second example is the emotion of being relaxed.

So to help determine the emotion that you put in your answer to WIIFM, consider a feature of your product or service and then think of the benefit that comes out of that feature. Again, remember "***Features Tell & Benefits Sell***"

What's In It For Me?
26 ~ *Answering That Question* ~ 26

by
David K. Ewen, M.Ed.

Practice: Features & Benefits

	FEATURES of Product / Service	BENEFITS resulting from Features	EMOTION from Benefit
1			
2			
3			
4			
5			

What's In It For Me?
27 ~ *Answering That Question* ~ 27

by
David K. Ewen, M.Ed.

More Practice

Remember: Features TEll & **Benefits SELL**

	FEATURES of Product / Service	BENEFITS resulting from Features	EMOTION from Benefit
1			
2			
3			
4			
5			

What's In It For Me?
28 ~ *Answering That Question* ~ 28

by
David K. Ewen, M.Ed.

Practice

We defined previously the definition of WIIFM. Write that down and perhaps some guiding notes if you need that. The next step is to use this model to brainstorm. Take time to come up with ideas.

Remember, the WIIFM model is the answer to a question that has an affirmation, a definitive, that speaks directly to your audience.

For the "Emotion", remember to first identify features that in turn produce a benefit. Let that benefit be an emotion.

WIIFM

- SIMPLE SUBJECT
- DEFINITIVE
- BYPRODUCT OR END RESULT OF WHAT IS BEING DELIVERED. SPOKEN IN TERMS OF EMOTION

WIIFM = (It/This) will (Make/Give) you _Emotion_

- WIIFM = WHAT'S IN IT FOR ME
- AFFIRMATION
- SPEAKING DIRECTLY TO CUSTOMER

What's In It For Me?
~ Answering That Question ~

by
David K. Ewen, M.Ed.

Practice Sheet

WIIFM=(It/This) will (Make/Give) you _(emotion)_

	subject, affirmation, definitive	emotion
1	It will make you ...	
2	This will give you ...	
3	It will give you ...	
4	This will make you ...	

Copyright © 2006, Ewen Prime Company
All rights reserved.

What's In It For Me?
30 ~ *Answering That Question* ~ 30

by
David K. Ewen, M.Ed.

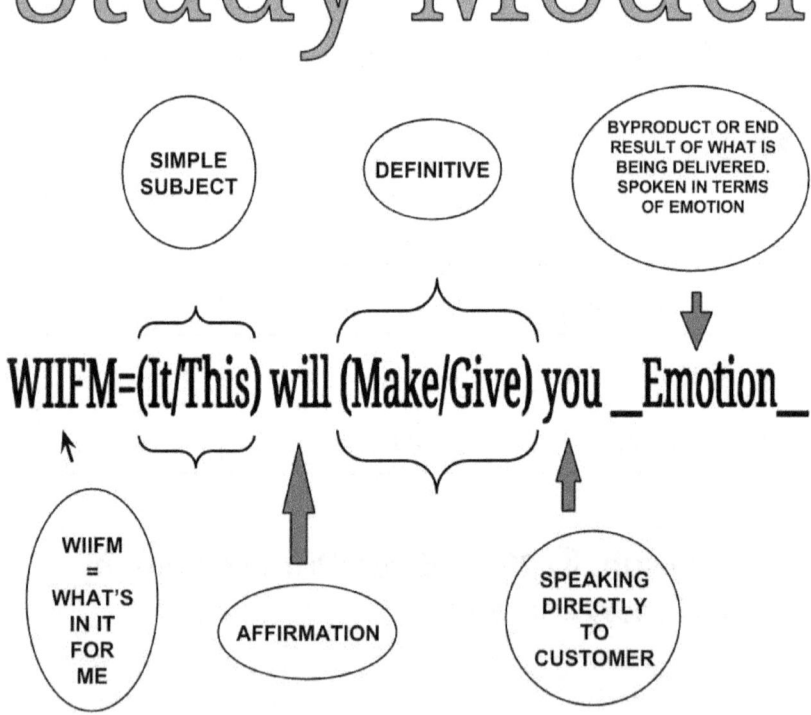

What's In It For Me?
31 ~ *Answering That Question* ~ 31

by
David K. Ewen, M.Ed.

More Practice

WIIFM=(It/This) will (Make/Give) you _(emotion)_

	subject, affirmation, definitive	emotion
1	It will make you ...	
2	This will give you ...	
3	It will give you ...	
4	This will make you ...	

Copyright © 2006, Ewen Prime Company
All rights reserved.

What's In It For Me?
32 ~ *Answering That Question* ~ 32

by
David K. Ewen, M.Ed.

Conclusion

You now have a model to work with to help answer the question from your client or customer "What's In It For Me?". Insight has been given as to how your client or customer thinks. Take advantage of the model to more effectively talk about your product or service.

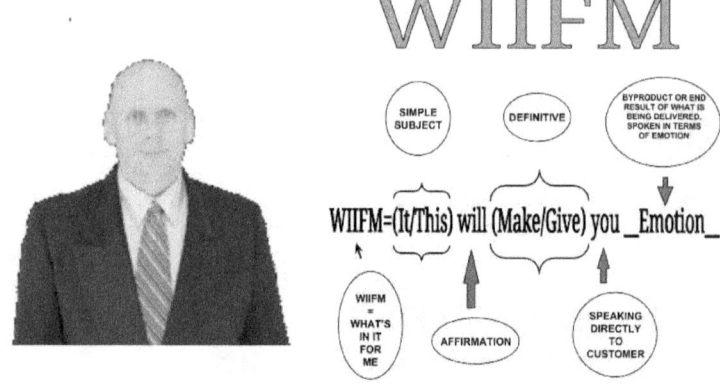

What's In It For Me?
33 ~ *Answering That Question* ~ 33

by
David K. Ewen, M.Ed.

What's In It For Me?
Answering That Question
By
David K. Ewen, M.Ed.

Copyright © 2013, Ewen Prime Company,

ALL RIGHTS RESERVED. This book contains material protected under International and Federal Copyright Laws and Treaties. Any unauthorized reprint or use of this material is prohibited. No part of this book may be reproduced or transmitted in any form or by any means, electronic or mechanical, including photocopying, recording, or by any information storage and retrieval system without express written permission from Ewen Prime Company, Inc.

www.ingramcontent.com/pod-product-compliance
Lightning Source LLC
Chambersburg PA
CBHW051827170526
45167CB00005B/2191